Heroic witness and prophet

A woman of great courage and strength, with a deep love of Christ and the Church, Marthe Louise Robin was born on 13 March 1902 at Châteauneuf-de-Galaure, near Lyons in south-eastern France; she died there on 6 February 1981, aged 78, having been bedridden and almost totally paralysed or more than half a century.

Marthe Robin was a straightforward countrywoman with a gentle and witty turn of phrase, ready always to listen to anyone and advise them where to turn in their hour of need. She spoke easily and knowledgeably of prayer, of God, of Jesus, and of the Blessed Virgin Mary. She was widely loved and greatly revered, and her funeral in 1981 was attended by thousands of mourners, including six bishops and more than 200 priests. During her lifetime and in the years since, her message and example and her spiritual fervour and encouragement have given great inspiration and direction to many men and women, of all ages and from all walks of life.

She had a particularly deep and burning devotion to Our Lady, and tried to live in the closest union with Christ, dedicating her sufferings to him and ready to share fully in his passion and death. In October 1930, she received the stigmata, the marks of the passion, and each Friday thereafter she underwent the most racking and intense pains of his death on the Cross.

In her prayers, Our Lord revealed a vision of a new Pentecost of love. God's call was for the renewal of the Church, through the apostolate of consecrated lay men and women living together in communities of prayer and work. The communities would be called 'Foyers de Lumière, de Charité et d'Amour' - centres or homes of light, charity and love. This was Marthe Robin's principal message: we must follow Jesus with the help and power of Mary.

During her life, Marthe met tens of thousands of people who visited her at home in the small room to which she was confined for most of her life. She spent around ten minutes with each visitor, enjoying an open and free conversation that often shed light on a person's problem or concern and always ended with a simple prayer.

In addition to those men and women she met at her bedside, she dealt with an unending flow of letters, despite losing her sight when she was only 38. She left a quantity of influential spiritual writings, and many of her insights, inspirations and instructions were written down by Père

MARTHE ROBIN

A CHOSEN SOUL

An Anthology

Père Michel Tierney, Martin Blake and David Fanning

All booklets are published thanks to the generous support of the members of the Catholic Truth Society

CATHOLIC TRUTH SOCIETY
PUBLISHERS TO THE HOLY SEE

Contents

Acknowledgements

CTS is grateful to **Editions Le Livre Ouvert** for their kind permission to publish the English language translation of **'Marthe
Robin, une âme d'élite'** by Père Michel Tierny, included here as
'Marthe Robin, A Chosen Soul' and translated by Martin
Blake. CTS thanks David Fanning for his kind permission to
include his work **'Marthe Robin, Charity and Love'.** Thanks
are also due to Martin Blake for supervising the collection and
ordering of the material gathered here.

Georges Finet, her spiritual director and co-founder of the worldwide network of Foyers de Charité.

Her writings and spiritual counsel both illuminated the problems and challenges facing the Catholic Church in her own lifetime and foreshadowed today's calls for evangelisation and renewal and for more lay involvement in the Church.

She was one of the most inspiring women of the present century, a rare and heroic witness to the passion and death of Jesus Christ, an extraordinary Christian and, in the words of one of her biographers, 'a treasure of the Church'.

Childhood

Joseph and Amélie Robin were simple peasant farmers, with a small farm on a plateau in the valley of the Galaure river in the Drôme department of south-eastern France. On Thursday, 13 March 1902, two weeks before Easter, their sixth child was born: Marthe Louise, a sister for Célina, the eldest daughter then aged 13, Gabrielle, Alice, Clémence and Henri, the only boy. Three weeks later, on the first Saturday in April, Marthe was baptised in the parish church of St Bonnet-de-Galaure; her brother Henri, aged 6, was her godfather and her sister Alice, aged 8, was her godmother.

Illness and tragedy struck the Robin family the year after Marthe's birth; a typhoid fever epidemic caused the death of Clémence, then aged 5, and seriously affected Marthe, whose health thereafter remained fragile.

The young Marthe was a cheerful and happy child, always willing to do whatever was asked of her and thoughtful of others. The marriage of her sister Célina in 1908 was a particularly joyous occasion for the six-year-old Marthe, who danced enthusiastically and joined in the celebrations to the full. She began school that year also, walking two kilometres each morning and evening with her sisters to the village school at Châteauneuf-de-Galaure. More often than not she arrived late, her poor health slowing her down, and her studies suffered.

At the age of 10, she made her first Holy Communion and this marked a turning point in her life; she was to say later that she believed that Our Lord had taken possession of her at that moment. Marthe was a prayerful child, praying to the Holy Spirit as often as she could, but usually in secret, particularly in her bed at night. Her rosary beads were her constant companion: 'When I went to the village on errands, I always had my beads in my pocket, and I said the rosary as I went along'.

She left school at 14, without any educational certificates, and settled into the normal day-to-day life of a young French peasant girl of her age, working in the house and in the fields. She was happy and content with her life and her family, enjoying the countryside and the companionship of her brother and sisters. They also had the friendship of neighbouring families, and the youngsters were in and out of each other's homes all the time. Marthe joined in with all the gusto of carefree youth, laughing, singing, dancing, and telling funny stories. She enjoyed real happiness.

Suffering

Two years later, her health deteriorated and she began to endure severe headaches. One day in November 1918, she fell in the house and was unable to raise herself. Partially paralysed and stricken by a debilitating and mysterious illness (possibly some form of sleeping sickness or inflammation of the brain), she spent the following thirty months in a near comatose state, obviously in pain and suffering, crying out on occasions. She hardly moved or spoke, she ate practically nothing, and she dozed virtually all the time. It was thought that she would die and in April 1921, aged 19, she received the last rites of the Church. To everyone's astonishment, she rallied instantly and demanded to get up.

Marthe recovered her strength slowly and could walk only with the aid of sticks. She spent a great part of the next eight years quietly embroidering baby clothes, reading, and praying, sitting in an armchair in the kitchen. In the spring of 1922, she was looking after her sister Gabrielle's house nearby, while Gabrielle was absent in Marseilles. Poking around in the attic, Marthe opened an old trunk and found a book of religious reflections (maybe, *'The Secret of Mary'*, by St Louis de Montfort.) Two phrases in the book made an immediate impression on her: 'Your way will be one of suffering' and 'One must give God everything'. Shortly after this, Marthe's health worsened again. Her eyesight weakened and she could walk now only with great difficulty. It was arranged that she should go on the diocesan pilgrimage to Lourdes, but at the last minute Marthe gave up her place in favour of a sick person from a neighbouring village.

Marthe offered her suffering to Christ, and on 15 October 1925 when she was 23, she set down the first of her spiritual writings, many of which were dictated to various women friends and are regarded as family treasures by members of the Foyers.

In 'Consécration Totale de Victime d'Amour', an act of complete abandonment to the will of God, she wrote at length about love and made herself a living sacrifice to God: 'O adorable Saviour! You are the unique possessor of my soul and of all my being! Receive the sacrifice that each day and at every moment I offer you in silence'. She dedicated her prayers and suffering to 'the good of the millions of hearts that do not love you, for the conversion of sinners, for the return of those who have gone astray and the infidels, for the holiness and apostolate of all your well-loved priests, and for all creatures'. From that time on, Marthe had one overwhelming objective in life: to offer herself entirely to God.

Surrender

In October 1926, she became seriously ill once more and was again given the last sacraments. Marthe had long been a lover of Thérèse Martin, the saintly Carmelite nun of Lisieux who had died in 1897 at the aged of 24 and whose 'little way' of simple, childlike and trusting Christianity had become so popular throughout France. Thérèse had been canonised in 1925 and now appeared to Marthe in three separate visions. The saint told Marthe that she was not going to die but that she would live and carry on Thérèse's mission, making it more universal.

About this time, Marthe said that 'suffering is the best school in which to learn true love' and she constantly offered her pain and her anguish to God. Eighteen months later, her legs became twisted and permanently paralysed; in her mind, God was simply taking what she had already offered him. A local carpenter made a small divan and it was placed in a downstairs bedroom; on that divan Marthe was to spend the rest of her life.

Soon afterwards, she lost the use of her hands. She was now paralysed from head to foot, unable to eat and drink, and without even the solace of sleep. The most her parents could do for her was to wash her and occasionally moisten her lips with water or coffee.

From then on, for the next fifty years until she died in 1981, the only sustenance taken by Marthe was the

Eucharist, which she received once a week, generally on a Wednesday. Her preparation for holy communion was intense. In the morning she reaffirmed her vows of October 1925, and appeared excited and eager; in the evening she would make her confession, an Act of Reconciliation, and then receive the Eucharist from the parish priest. She entered a state of ecstasy after receiving the Body of Christ, only returning to normal during the morning or afternoon of the following day.

Marthe was 28 when she received the stigmata, the marks of the passion of Christ on her hands, feet, body and head. It was the end of September 1930 when Jesus Christ appeared in a vision to Marthe and asked whether she wanted to be like him. Her reply was clear and immediate: 'Let the Lord's will be done!' Three days later, she was again visited by the crucified Jesus.

Passion

As she described later, she found herself raised in the air before Christ on the Cross. Her arms were stretched out towards the Cross, and a tongue of flame shot from Christ's heart, split into two forks and pierced Marthe's hands. In the same way, her crippled legs were straightened and the flames pierced her feet. She said she felt as if her life was being drawn from her. A dart of fire entered her chest and encircled and pierced her heart, which remained faint and aching for several hours. Then Christ pressed down his crown of thorns on her head.

Marthe said that Christ told her: 'Now I shall call you my little one, crucified with love. After my Mother, it is you who will live my Passion to the fullest'.

In the morning, Marthe's mother washed the blood from the young woman's body. The marks of the crucifixion were to remain for the rest of Marthe's life, and she regularly shed drops of blood from the wounds.

Thereafter, on the Friday of each week she relived the passion of Christ. From time to time, as she endured Christ's torment in her own body, she would call out his words from the cross and ask God for help and relief. Then, late in the afternoon she would let out a strange cry before her head fell backwards on the bed, as if she had died. Marthe would remain in that state for several hours, and be quiet for the next day or two.

Though Marthe would cry out and pray aloud during the weekly passions until around 1948, after that time each week's events took place in absolute silence. It was as if she were fully united in Christ and in a secret place.

A modest and unassuming woman, Marthe refused to speak of the passions and torments that marked her life and never mentioned the stigmata and the blood that flowed from those wounds. She did not talk about not eating or drinking or about not sleeping. All these were things to be lived as part of her complete surrender to the will and love of Christ.

In December 1930 Marthe described her profound joy
and deep happiness despite the intensity of her sufferings,
which were 'bearable because sacred'. She continued:
'When the thorns are many, Jesus supports me more
closely, so that I may continue in spite of the wounds;
confidence and courage! Jesus makes himself so loving
and so good for a little soul covered in blood'. Marthe followed Christ without resistance.

Apostolate

The news of Marthe's intimate union with Christ soon
spread around the district, and beyond. Villagers and their
families began to come to see her, organised and mar-
shalled by the parish priest and her family.

People came to tell her their problems and ask for
Marthe's advice and prayers. The visitors lined up patiently
in the small farmhouse kitchen, waiting their turn, priest and
layman alike. She particularly enjoyed the visits of the children who came after school and at weekends or in the school
holidays. The young boys and girls were her favourite visitors, and she listened to their stories and said the rosary with
them. She encouraged them gently and wisely and spoke to
them of hope and of the love of God. For her, the children
were the closest to Christ; they were God's 'treasures' and
'we must show them how much we love them'.

One of her particular gifts was the composition of powerful and beautiful prayers, and she knew well the power of

prayer and how often it was answered. There are several instances of children in particular being saved through the intercession of prayer.

Marthe began to see that she had been singled out by Jesus to help in a grand project that He had for the world.

It was in the early 1930's that she initiated the first step in a worldwide endeavour that continues to be extended and become more and more established. It was revealed to her that the local community needed a Christian school and she urged the parish priest to do all he could to open one. Initially, the priest was discouraging; after all, in a strongly secular village, why should anyone send children to a church school? Marthe persisted, however, and eventually the priest's resistance crumbled. He was able to buy cheaply the neglected local château and, after some renovation and preparation, the new school opened in October 1934, with two teachers and just seven pupils.

Over the years since, that small village school has grown into a major girls' school (with several hundred students between the ages of 5 and 18), with a separate boys' school in the neighbouring village of St Bonnet and an agricultural college nearby. From the first seven schoolchildren in 1934, the three colleges now cater for more than a thousand students.

For the school, Marthe wanted a special picture of the Blessed Virgin Mary. After reading St Louis de

Montfort's *'The Secret of Mary'*, most of which she knew by heart, she had been visited by Mary several times and spoke to her daily. Mary was the ideal, full of God's grace, mother of God and queen of Heaven. Marthe commissioned a painting of Mary, Mediatrix of all Graces, from a painter in Lyons.

Père Georges Finet, a priest from Lyons, brought the picture to Marthe at Châteauneuf on 10 February 1936 and spent around three hours with her. It was a visit that changed his life and set in train the next steps in Marthe's work for Christ.

The priest had long had a special devotion to Mary and admired the works of St Louis de Montfort. In listening to Marthe talk about Mary, about the modern Church and the world, and about the total rejuvenation of the Church, he realised that here was a particularly rare soul, a 'pure marvel'. To his astonishment, Marthe told him that she had a task for him from God; 'It is you who are to come here to Châteauneuf to found the first Foyer of Charity'.

The concept of a spiritual centre (or *'foyer'*) bursting and resounding with light, charity and love, a place where lay men and women could attend week-long retreats and where members of the Foyer could return to the practices and values of the Church of the first centuries after Christ's birth and death, had been revealed by Our Lord to Marthe in 1933.

Marthe tells of how Jesus spoke to her 'of the splendid 'work' which he wished to realise here to the glory of the Father, for the extension of his reign in the whole Church, and for the renewal of the entire world' and how he asked for her personal participation in that work. She was anxious as to how she could possibly collaborate in such a great enterprise. 'Do not be afraid', she was told, 'I shall do everything'. Christ said that he would send a priest to start the work and bring it to fruition. Three years later, he sent the Abbé Finet.

Foyers de Charité

Under the direction of a priest, baptized and consecrated adult men and women live together in community, sharing their material, intellectual and spiritual assets. The members of the Foyer community collaborate with each other and with the priest in an apostolic activity and seek to bear witness, through their lives, their prayers and their work, to the light, charity and love of Christ. They have a common vocation to charity.

The community reveals the Gospel, spreading the Word of God, welcoming all men and women, offering both spiritual and practical help, without favour and without question.

For lay people and religious, the Foyers offer programmes of retreats, principally for adults although whole families, including young people, may attend. Each retreat is centred on a single theme, and all offer the opportunity to listen to and understand the Word of God, while living simply and in silence.

The first retreat began on 7 September 1936 in the girls' school at Châteauneuf-de-Galaure. The second retreat was held three months later. Since then, the network of Foyers has spread around the world and their activities and following have multiplied greatly.

Today, the Foyer at Châteauneuf has more than 100 people living in the community and there is room for a further 200 or so retreatants, including a special wing for young children.

There are currently 70 Foyers worldwide: in Europe (16 in France), Africa, Central and South America, North America, the West Indies and in Asia. While there is, as yet, no Foyer established in the British Isles, there is a growing awareness of Marthe and her work and message and a strengthening intention to set up a Foyer of Charity in Britain. Each year, many men and women from Britain and Ireland attend retreats at one or other of the Foyers in France. Several Foyers run schools, playing a significant part in the religious formation of the young, an apostolate to which Marthe gave special importance.

In November 1975, Pope Paul VI said of the Foyers: 'The Foyers provide genuine doctrinal and spiritual instruction, in an atmosphere of silence, of charity, and of devotion to Mary that opens souls to conversion, having made their lives fuller with God...'

Fidelity

From the date of his first meeting with Marthe in 1936, Père Finet was close to her for forty-five years and he experienced great and extraordinary moments alongside simple and everyday occurrences. It was a relationship perhaps unique in Church history.

Marthe had become blind in 1940, offering her sight to Our Lord for peace and the conversion of France, but this in no way interfered with her work on God's behalf. As she said, she drew love from the heart of Christ and gave it away to all those who visited her and to the many thousands who wrote to her.

Her mission was to put men and women everywhere in touch with God and with one another. She prayed earnestly and often for the Church's renewal. Though just a 'small and inactive and weak' person, as she called herself, she was the instrument of God's will and through her Père Finet and countless others were called to serve in a remarkable missionary apostolate.

Towards the end of her life, Marthe continued to be tested severely and her final years were marked by yet more pain and suffering. In November 1980 her spine became permanently and most painfully twisted, and a few weeks later she developed a harrowing cough that did not leave her.

Marthe could no longer speak or see, and she was in constant torment and pain. Visitors were forbidden as her condition worsened. At the beginning of February 1981 she told Père Finet that her time on earth was coming to an end, and she asked that her family gather round her. On the Wednesday, surrounded by a good many of her family, she received Holy Communion; the following day, she endured her final participation in Christ's passion, coming out of it late in the evening. In the afternoon of Friday, 6 February 1981, Marthe died.

Dressed like a first communicant, in a clean white gown, the body of Marthe lay on the bed to which she had been confined for most of her life. Her face appeared radiantly happy and peaceful yet strong and forceful; pain and suffering, even death, had been beaten and Marthe had entered fully into her life with Christ.

On Tuesday, 10 February 1981, her body was placed in a coffin and taken from the farmhouse where she had spent all her life. The coffin was removed to the new Foyer chapel, which she had never been able to visit.

Two days later, the funeral took place at the Foyer. Mourners came by road and by special trains from all over France and from overseas. Priests and bishops celebrated the requiem mass, and some six thousand people received the Eucharist. After Mass, the coffin was transported to St Bonnet-de-Galaure, and Marthe was buried, quietly, in the Robin family burial plot.

At the funeral mass, the Bishop of Valence spoke warmly of Marthe's life and suffering, of her dedication and her joy. 'All of us must fill our niches in the Church, with our own gifts, qualities, and thirst for God. Marthe filled hers - she filled it very well indeed'.

Marthe Robin may seem a mystery, a daunting example to follow. She lost virtually all her physical capacities one after another, and became wholly dependent on other people, living to die so that she might be with God or ever. To many, her life and destiny were extraordinary. In truth, though, she was a simple person, a loving child of God and a loyal daughter of the Church, for whom life meant Christ. She was an exemplary Christian.

Marthe spoke often about a new Pentecost of love, when the Church would be renewed by an apostolate of the laity, who were going to take an increasingly important part in the Church. Asked about this, she replied that she saw it as nothing extraordinary. 'I see it as something peaceful, coming slowly. I think it will come little by little. As for the future, you know people claim all sorts of ideas about the future from me, but I only know one thing for certain: the future is Jesus'.

A Meeting with Marthe Robin

by Yves de Boisredon

I was born into a believing family. My parents told me that they prayed for me even before I was born; we always prayed 'en famille' morning and evening, and at meals.

At about the age of 16 or 17, I was seized by a crazy dream. I was going to makes lots of money, so that by the age of 40 I would be rich enough to do whatever I liked with my life. My studies at school had been no more than mediocre, but I threw myself into minor business activities which began to reap rewards. A few years later I was offered a job in a wine exporting business with the prospect that if I was successful I might become the boss. And that is what happened. So I began to lead the life of a businessman travelling around the world for eight months of the year, and reaping whatever advantage I could. In material terms I had everything I had dreamt of... I hunted, piloted aeroplanes, and so on; and mothers of eligible daughters held me in high marital esteem.

But my personal life was becoming seriously downgraded. I was totally indifferent to everything regarding the Faith. I drank more than was good for me. I was smoking at least fifty cigarettes a day. A doctor friend told me one day that if I carried on that way I should risk damaging my brain. This scared me to the extent that I agreed to go away for a complete rest after the end of a planned business trip.

Doctor's orders

On my return the doctor rang me up. "Yves, you remember your promise? Well, I've found just the place for you". I waited for a description of some plush five-star hotel with swimming-pool, golf course, etc. "Its called Châteauneuf-de-Galaure; its a Foyer of Charity, a place where people make retreats".

"But I've no wish to make a retreat!"

"I know; but do go just the same. The whole thing is in silence, and you don't have to attend the talks if you don't want to; the food is good and the place is comfortable. Its really the ideal place for a rest cure!"

So I found myself booked for a retreat! That was in July 1980. I arrived one Monday evening and settled into my room with the intention of sleeping as much as possible. However, next morning I awoke feeling fresh at seven o'clock, and with no desire to go back to sleep. So I got up and decided to attend the first conference after breakfast.

It was Père Finet who was giving the talks. I was quickly struck by the fact that it was perfectly clear that he was a priest. What was more he said things with intelligence and humour which rang true. Lunchtime came.

While we were at table another priest took the mike and began to talk about a person called Marthe Robin who was marked with the stigmata of Our Lord's Passion and who every week relived this experience. This puzzled me. But I went to the next conference in the course of which Père Finet warned us against the temptation to pack up and leave. Cut to the quick, I decided I must remain, come what may.

We were told we might put our names down on a list to visit Marthe, with the proviso that, being a large number, we might not all be able to meet her. I put my name down partly out of curiosity, reckoning that since I was never lucky at gambling, I would probably not be one to see her. The retreat went on. On Wednesday I went to confession, a reflex from my school retreats. I found Père Finet and went to him. I have the impression that this lasted only about three minutes and I have no precise recollection of it. But I do remember seeing Rembrandt's 'Prodigal Son' some time later, and thinking that this picture of the tenderness of the Father for his child was exactly what I had experienced during this confession.

Visit to Marthe

Thursday came, which was the last possible day to see Marthe; and there was my name on the list. Rather anxiously I arrived at 'La Plaine', not knowing too well what I was going to say to her. I waited in the kitchen. When my

turn came I went into her darkened room and sat on the little chair beside her couch.

"Bonjour!"

"Bonjour... My name is Yves de Boisredon. I'm 33 and
I export wine".

"Ah yes... are you enjoying the retreat?"

"Yes. I like Père Finet a lot".

"Do you know the Foyers of Charity?"

I told her how I had gone one year to the Port-au-Prince
Foyer for the Midnight Mass. Then she said:

"You know at your age you should be contemplating
marriage or the priesthood or consecrated celibacy".

I can hear myself replying: "Can one be thinking of the
priesthood at the age of 33?" Marthe then asked me what
studies I had done, and whether I had ever learnt Latin or
Greek. Then she said:

"You know you can't wait ten years or you will be
'driving alongside your own road'. Now would you like to
pray with me?"

I knelt beside her bed and heard her begin the Hail
Mary in a voice of extraordinary tenderness. At that
moment tears came gushing from my eyes. I could not
believe one could cry like that, yet at the same time I felt
no embarrassment. At the end of the prayer I murmured
a goodbye. She answered with: "Goodbye, and thank
you". I went out into the courtyard and there had an
experience which it is difficult to describe, extremely

sweet and powerful. The best way to speak of it is to evoke the episode of the rich young man in the Gospel: "Jesus looked at him and loved him". I put my head in my hands and said to myself: "Yves, you're a priest!" Tears poured forth abundantly, but I felt an extraordinary peace and joy. This was accompanied by total certainty and security; nothing and no one would be able to remove that peace from me.

My vocation

Having said this, however, my brain started to react violently. "But you're going crazy... a rascal like you has never turned into a priest!" I decided I must see Père Finet as soon as possible. There was a long queue waiting at his door! Next day the same thing. I went on following the retreat; each time I saw a priest or heard the priesthood mentioned tears welled into my eyes. On Friday there was a whole conference on the subject, and I got through most of my Kleenex.

Finally at mid-day on the Sunday I managed to speak to him. He gave me an appointment for the afternoon. I told him what had happened.

"Well its quite simple", he said, "you are going to become a priest. You will do the necessary studies, and all will go well. And now I will give you my blessing". We fell into each others arms, and I began to cry again, and he blessed me.

Fifteen months later I entered the seminary. There I met members of the Emmanuel Community, to which I soon felt called. Community life was a great support on my journey towards ordination. This took place in June 1987 in the diocese of Paris. I was then 40.

(This encounter took place in July 1980. Marthe died in February of the following year. Yves would therefore be amongst the last retreatants to have met her, as for several months before her death she was unable to have visitors). *(Translated from the magazine 'Il est Vivant' of January 1991 by Martin Blake).*

Prayer for Priests

Take your priests, O my God, fully and entirely, to accomplish or at least help to accomplish all that You wish of them. Lead them in everything and for everything. Be their strength, O my God. May all their action, whether important or unimportant, come to them from You, depend on You, and be addressed to You. May they be all for You, O my God, to glorify You, to love You and to make You loved. My God, set our hearts on fire with your Love; fill us with your Divine Joy. O Father, spread throughout the world and over souls your supreme Mercy and your divine Pardon. My God, show your Love to France and to the whole world; re-establish peace and order on earth. Lead all people to unity, O my God, and unite their spirits and hearts in You.

MARTHE ROBIN: A CHOSEN SOUL

by Père Michel Tierny

Marthe Robin, "the little peasant of the Drôme", was born on 13 March 1902 at Châteauneuf-de-Galaure.

The Lord "took possession of her heart" at her First Communion and her love for Him grew steadily until in 1930, at the age of 28, she was brought into total union with Him by means of the stigmata.

On 6 February 1981, she left this world after a long life of fidelity in the offering of her sufferings united to Jesus.

Her union with Jesus Christ gives meaning and fruitfulness to Marthe's life. She lived as a Carmelite contemplative in the little farmhouse where she was born.

For fifty years she offered herself completely in a hidden manner, never leaving the couch on which she lay in her parents' house. Like Saint Thérèse she was to be "a missionary of love".

The Foyers of Charity were born in 1936 from her meeting with Père Finet, and they are now spread throughout the whole world.

A Foyer of Charity seeks to allow men and women to hear the Word of God in an atmosphere of interior recollection, and to meditate on it fruitfully.

Marthe's hallmark was an extraordinary humanism which fidelity to God produced in her, in the greatest simplicity.

United to the Passion and Resurrection of Christ -

"Most perfect Mother, all powerful and all good, in my sincere desire to conform fully and faithfully to the design of God, I beg you to help me and to make of my life the masterpiece of love which He expects and desires".

"A chosen soul"

With these words Abbé Faure, the parish priest of Châteauneuf, introduced his parishioner to Abbé Finet on 10 February 1936. Apparently she was not a 'chosen soul' in any usual sense, as having special gifts. Marthe has indicated to us the meaning of her life: "My joy is to live quite hidden in God with Christ, to lose myself in Him and to allow myself to be 'taken over'. That is how the Blessed Virgin lived; and she will remain my living and incomparable model to the very end".

"As an infinitely good Father, God has prepared from all eternity a mission for every soul; our task is to let ourselves be taken over, and to give ourselves when He calls us, and not to impose ourselves".

Those who met her at La Plaine (her farmhouse) never saw anything extraordinary, and yet how many lives were enlightened, strengthened, sometimes even changed there, after a simple dialogue with this ordinary woman. Often it was only later that they discovered the truth and depth of her influence.

The secret of her joy was her union with Jesus. Just as the Mother of God was greeted by the Angel as "full of grace", so neither did Marthe choose her vocation. She received and discovered it, and accepted it through a series of events in which she gradually recognised the hand of God, with the help of the Holy Spirit. "It would be so sad to receive everything from Love and not to give everything to Love. Isn't it the ideal of the Christian to be taken over by Christ? Ah, if only we were to love Jesus as He has loved us!"

"Let us allow God to make use of us as instruments of his Word and his will. Nothing is small for the greater glory of God. To work for Him in all things is to serve humbly a great cause. Thus may nothing remain unproductive within our hands".

1902-1918: the choice of God in a normal childhood

"I always loved God as a little girl"

Born on 13 March 1902 near a small village in the Drôme Department called Châteauneuf-de-Galaure, Marthe was the youngest of a family of six children. All her life she remained devoted to her family, and above all to her parents who were modest farmers, who brought her up in the faith of the Church and implanted in her a taste for simplicity of life. This family life may have been rough and ready at times, but perseverance in work, the experience of service and sharing, together with the simple celebration of joys and troubles with neighbours and kinsfolk, gave it profound meaning. As a child Marthe showed great consideration for others, a spontaneous readiness to render service, and an affectionate understanding of her friends, as well as a certain attraction towards the poor and the sick. "I would have crossed hills and valleys, had I been allowed, to go and see a sick friend, not to look after him but to love him".

This tenderness of heart expressed itself in a joyful nature, lively and sometimes even mischievous. She went happily to school and catechism classes with the other village children. After school she would help in the house or on the farm. And through these ordinary experiences she discovered the presence of the Saviour and little by little a deep attraction for Him.

Recalling her first Communion she said later: "I think Our Lord took possession of me then; I believe He took

me for himself at that moment. My first Communion was
something very sweet in my life". Theologians may recognise in these words the expression of 'passiveness' proper
to mystics; Marthe was conscious of being loved in a
unique way, with a love both strong and true, whose
sweetness was equalled by strength.

Like Bernadette, she came to intimacy with Jesus by
praying the rosary and by discovering the closeness of
Her whom later she was to refer to as "Maman chérie".
The faith of a child no doubt, but already personal; "my
sisters didn't like my praying all the time, but I used
chiefly to pray in bed. I prayed to the Blessed Virgin; I
used to talk to her. When I went down to the village on
errands I always carried a rosary in my pocket and used
to say it as I walked along. I prayed more in thought
than in words".

No doubt it was at this age that Marthe sowed in her
memory the divine seeds of the Word of God, and above
all the Gospels in which lay hidden, she was to say, the
secret for always being happy. These words soon became
for her the 'Book of Books'. "It was through this book that
the Lord taught me all I know and have to say, and from
the Tabernacle where He speaks to me, He nourished me
when I was hungry for such good and beautiful things,
which surpass description".

"Sickness is a wonderful grace, an incomparable richness. Ah! May the grace of suffering reveal such beauty and teach such great things!"
"It was in His Holy Passion and in suffering that Christ came closest to our human weakness; it is in pain that He brings us closest to Himself, and takes us into His most intimate company".

1918-1925: First challenges - first calls

"Lord, I bless you for testing me"

In 1918 Marthe was sixteen. She had already known delicate health in her childhood. Now she was to embark on a road of suffering which would only end at death. But if sickness came as a surprise to the adolescent, filled with desire, she did not rebel against it. Already the Holy Spirit murmured within her, "God is always there. It is He who allows everything which happens, even when He seems to be hiding and denying us; yet He always loves us". And she was able to pray: "With your grace I shall be strong and triumph, not on account of this trial, if that is what You will, but by this trial I belong to God".

"To his close friends God is pleased to speak quite quietly. He likes the soul who listens and speaks to it noiselessly... In love, what is said in a low voice has infinitely more value than what is

shouted out loud and is much better understood. To live within one's soul... All the divine lights are there! To pray within...".

It was an illness difficult to define, and for the doctors difficult to treat. It was marked by a long period of silence; for twenty-seven months Marthe lay as if paralysed, eating little and hardly speaking at all. What was happening between Marthe and Jesus at this time? We cannot tell. Père Finet commented later: "certainly a long intimacy", without amplification. We may however er believe that through what might appear from the outside as a curious incident, the Lord was forming her soul in a special way, for later on she said: "Resting on my faith and His all-powerfulness, and strengthened by the love of Him who can do all and who favours some with His divine help while at the same time preparing them for a Mission, I had the honour of realising the extent of His designs on me, in spite of my powerlessness, incapacities and weaknesses, with the assurance in my mind that He is able to do infinitely more than I can explain, want or understand".

It was then too that Marthe discovered the value of that silence "in which one hears the voice of God". That silence was to be for her a long period of prayer, and a secret preparation for the fifty year life of solitude in the little room where she spent whole days and nights in intimate union with God whom she named her "sweet Well-Beloved". When Marthe proposed the work of Retreats in the Foyers of Charity she was to insist greatly on the importance of silence, looked at not so much as an exercise in asceticism but as a necessary condition for listening to the Holy Spirit who speaks in the intimacy of the heart, "the divine silence of Love".

"How good silence is, and fruitful with God", she was to say later; "it is union with infinite love..." the silence of contemplation when the Word of God unveils its unfathomable riches.

It must have been during that period of her life that Marthe heard the Lord say clearly: "I have infinite plans for you", while at the same time she was to discover also that "between God and man there is a Calvary, and it is by the Cross that one has to climb as far as God". And as if the keynote for a mission, she kept recalling the sentence she found one day in an old book: "For you will be the way of suffering".

For Marthe, however, who felt within herself a bubbling vitality and who wanted so much to give the full measure of her being, it was never a question of suffering sought for its own sake, but suffering accepted out of love, so that she might be conformed to the Will of God, whom she wished to love and serve above all else. "What I should like to do and often dream of, is to please the good God without seeking myself or indeed anything else. What I desire above all is to love Him constantly, to love Him tenderly, to love Him without measure". This is the language of someone deeply in love with Him whose love she has come to recognise.

Yet the way forward was strewn with hesitations and resistances, even a certain conflict, since she spoke of years of anguish before she could give her unreserved 'Fiat', so often repeated thereafter. No doubt Marthe was coming to recognise the first attacks of the devil who never ceased from opposing her; at the same time she was also already favoured with an apparition of the Blessed Virgin.

"Jesus, I have seen Him moving across the world, laden with his Cross, searching for souls to bear it with Him; but they all ran away at his approach... so once more I offered myself..".

1925: Marthe's response of love.

"To be a victim of love for the Church and for souls" The hour for Marthe to choose had come. "It is not enough to have inspirations or blinding lights; one must respond to God's call." She would very much like to have entered Carmel. "We must give God everything".

She was thus ripe for abandoning herself entirely to the Lord, which she did in a decisive manner on 15 October 1925 by composing her 'Act of Abandonment and offering to the love and the Will of God'.

"Eternal God, infinite love, oh my Father! You have asked your little victim for everything; take then and receive everything... This day I give myself and consecrate myself to You, entirely and with no going back..."

"Of all the forms of the apostolate, that of good works, that of prayer, that of example, that of suffering, this last apostolate is worth the most; and prayer, like good works, only acquires its fruitfulness in sacrifice".

1925-1930: in the steps of St Thérèse
of the Child Jesus.

"From her holy convent, and especially from her small cell, the angelic little Thérèse of the Child Jesus has spread the graces of salvation to the ends of the earth by the heroism of her sacrifice. And that is why the Church, 'her good mother', has not hesitated to name her 'Patron of the Missions' and indeed refer to her as 'the greatest saint of modern times'." (And in 1998 she was proclaimed Doctor of the Church).

In October 1926, struck down once more by illness, Marthe fell into a coma for three weeks. In the course of this new silent trial St Thérèse appeared to her on three occasions, entrusting to her the continuation of her mission to the whole world. "Oh, the rascal", said Marthe

later, "she left everything to me!" Little by little she came
to understand that as a lay-person she was called to live
out her offering with the crucified Jesus, for the Church
and for the world.

"Lord, I am all yours; do what You will with me, and
since souls can only be won by suffering, continue your
Redeeming Passion in me".

On 25 March 1928 Marthe's legs became paralysed,
and she took to a divan from which she never rose again.
She could still embroider with needle and thread, and
write a few letters. She was the subject of violent attacks
by the devil, often followed by visions of Our Lady. In
February 1929 the paralysis spread to her arms and hands;
she was reduced to complete inactivity. Her Act of
Abandonment was being realised.

"No more of me... or of mine... or of anything... You
alone, Oh my Jesus. I renounce forever my own interests
and shall devote myself entirely to prayer, to suffering and
to Love".

**"To unite oneself to all to be united to God,
not to belong to God only for oneself... not to
be exclusive. If there are times of solitude with
God that nothing must interrupt, there are also
intimate moments with God which are real
meetings with people in the world. Don't let's
look only at our souls, we must look around and**

above. The work of God in souls is vast... each soul on earth may become a chosen one!. You have undergone the sacrifice to be loved by men; since it is necessary I will suffer martyrdom to make You loved by souls and to grow in love in order to be loved by You and to make You loved and known by everyone; at each blow of the chisel and hammer I shall say 'thank you'. I want to sweat love. Crown me with thorns, let my hands bleed, let my heart bleed, leave me on the Cross".

1930: Identified with Jesus crucified.

"I want to become totally Jesus, and Jesus crucified in order to become Jesus Redeemer..."

At the end of September 1930, Jesus appeared to Marthe and asked her: "Do you want to be like me?" Early in October she saw Jesus on the Cross asking the same question. It was the hour when the Bridegroom chose to unite himself more intimately with his bride, whom He knew to be ready to receive in her body the marks of his wounds and with the crown of thorns, like the seal of his love. "Madness for pagans; the wisdom of God". No more than the cross of Christ can the stigmata be understood outside the context of love.

It was for the love of his Father that Jesus accepted to go as far as death on the cross. It was because Marthe loved Jesus, and in Him loved the same will of the Father, that she was led to resemble Him in the very act by which He gave the world the greatest proof of his love.

"Oh Jesus, you said no one took your life but You gave it freely. I beg of You to give us the courage to suffer and die like You, not because we are obliged to do so, like slaves, but freely in holiness and love; let me die so that they may have life". With St Paul she could say:

"With Christ I am fixed to the Cross".

The following Friday Marthe began to re-live the Passion of Jesus, at the conclusion of which, in an ecstasy, the Blessed Virgin appeared to her. Crucified in her body and in her heart, she was from then on to experience mysteriously every week the various stages of the Passion, from the Agony in the Garden until the final words of Christ from the Cross: "Father, into your hands I commend my spirit".

Completely paralysed she no longer ate, nor drank, nor slept. Her only food was the Eucharist in which her Well-Beloved gave her each week nourishment and life. Truly she could say with Jesus:

'My food is to do the Will of the Father'.

At the heart of this suffering, unknown to most people, was the act of thanksgiving in which she united herself with Jesus.

"I am a useless servant, yet I have at least the sublime joy of working and suffering for my God, of giving and drawing on my life drop by drop, not in triumphal glory, but in the daily obscurity of an inglorious agony, where humility risks nothing. And so every day I embrace the immense task entrusted to me by the Redeemer with fresh gratitude and joy, and I thank Him for having given me the gift of his cup and his crown, and of the nails of His Holy Cross, with such prodigy; for having so lovingly given me life in which to carry on his long and painful Agony and Passion; finally, for having so bountifully and profoundly imprinted in me His suffering and Eucharistic life".

"Let there be just one single soul in each home overflowing with God, and it will fill the whole house.
Beneath the radiance of its beautiful warmth, listening to its penetrating and persuasive voice, by the light of its pure clarity, the most hardened and fiercely enclosed hearts will open up:
God will enter and will overcome them".

1930-1934: first steps in a great Mission

"Love alone draws me. How I should like to communicate it to everyone.."

The influence of Marthe's mission was first felt in her parish, through the foundation of a school, for which she had asked her parish priest, as a request from Our Lady

herself, back in 1930. Marthe liked to recall how Our
Lord, too, spoke early on to her heart. She loved to have
visits from local children, to listen to them, pray the rosary
with them, and share in their sense of wonder. She recognised the presence of the Triune God dwelling in them,
and through them she came closer to the pure Heart of
Jesus, Child of the Father and Mary's Child, abandoned
and full of love. She believed profoundly in the power of
their prayer. "Have not the hearts of children been created
for praying and loving? "The prayer of children is all-
powerful with the Heart of God".

By this link with children Marthe identified herself
with the 'Little Way' of Saint Thérèse of the Child Jesus,
in a similar abandonment to the maternal power of Mary.
The creation of a girls school at Châteauneuf was but a
preparatory stage in a mission which was to overflow
beyond the boundaries of the parish. Indeed, Marthe
received from the Lord an increasingly precise intuition
that, starting with Châteauneuf, He would realise a 'Work
of Love' for the regeneration of the whole world, in which
the Blessed Virgin would fully exercise her role as Mother
and Mediatrix.

"Its creation will be a refuge for people in great human
distress who will come seeking consolation and hope; and
within the shelter of its walls will be the clear sign of my
Will and the moving appeal of my Heart to innumerable
sinners, who will come from every part of the world,

drawn by Me and my Mother, in search of Light and the healing of their ills in my divine forgiveness. I want it to be a Foyer radiant with Light, Charity and Love".

The Word of God would be preached there in fundamental teaching given during five day retreats, in silence, by a priest who would be the Father of a community of baptised lay people, living together as a family with Mary as their Mother. With Marthe and like her, the members of the Foyer would be called to carry on the Work of Redemption in the spirit of the Holy Family of Nazareth, offering themselves and their daily lives in the service of the retreatants. "I want all the members of the Foyers to be saints. Let them shine by the example of a profoundly supernatural life, by the unceasing practice of charity, by their devotion in the face of hardship, and finally by their giving themselves to each and everyone in a total offering to God".

"Humble little soul as I am, yet capable of something great, even very great, for the Church and for souls, for the priesthood of the whole world, which I am engaged by God himself to support, and for the whole of mankind".

1936: two priesthoods united for the same Offering.

"I wish to create something new and very great for Our Glory".

More than ever Marthe felt herself to be a daughter of the Church. She always wanted to act in union with her parish priest, conscious of the fact that her lay priesthood could only be exercised through that of the ordained priest. Besides the advice of Abbé Faure, who felt himself increasingly outdistanced by his parishioner, Marthe received advice and support from other priests on a number of occasions. But Our Lord had promised, when speaking of the 'Work of the Foyers', to send her a priest who would be, like her, specially chosen for this vocation.

On 10 February 1936, Marthe was visited by Abbé Georges Finet, who was an expert in the Lyon diocese on Marian spirituality following the teaching of Saint Louis-Marie Grignion de Montfort. At the end of an interview lasting three hours, she told him that he was chosen by God to become her 'Father' and the Father of the first Foyer of Charity, there at Châteauneuf. In the course of one of her 'Passions' Jesus had said to her: "The priest whom I shall send you will not be able to do anything without you nor far from you. I want you both to be united with Me for the Mission which I shall entrust to you, for all the souls which I want to give you, and for the glory of My Name".

Such a project naturally surprised Abbé Finet, but how could he not see the work of the Holy Spirit in this soul so humbly united to the Lord and so close to the Virgin Mary, to whom he too liked to entrust himself like a child. And so, with the agreement of his Bishop and the encouragement of several of his superiors, he went off to found the first Foyer of Charity at Châteauneuf-de-Galaure, and began the work of the retreats.

In the evening of the first day of the first retreat, 8 September 1936, Abbé Finet heard himself addressed by Marthe for the first time as "Père", and so was consecrated in his mission with her in the Foyer where he would be called upon to give supernatural life to so many children. Quite quickly a family formed around Père Finet, allowing many retreatants to be received, and soon the building of a new house, despite the difficulties of wartime, made this operation possible.

"... and you, my Father, standing each morning at the Altar, I beg you to offer the little host that I am to the great and divine Host on behalf of souls, so that with Jesus, through Jesus, and by Jesus, God may draw from His little host all the praise and glory which He expects from it, and for souls all the graces that they need".

"I have prayed ardently and with so much affection for my spiritual Father".

"Oh my God, bless my Father, bless all those he loves, bless all his works, and sanctify all his words. Bless his Foyer of Charity".

"I want to enlighten souls as did the Prophets and Doctors of the Church... I should like to go all over the earth in every direction, and preach the Holy Name of God, and plant in the ground the Glorious Cross of our Lord Jesus Christ. But one mission would not be enough...".

"God has given me the apostolate of love in suffering".

1936-1948: perseverance in the Offering

"To expiate, repair, console, love... to give and spend myself without reserve and with all my being for God, for others... for souls".

"The souls which the Lord has entrusted to me directly, and whom I want to fill with divine love, are so numerous..." In such close association with the Redeeming Work of Christ, Marthe was in communion with the very Heart of the Father "who wants all men to be saved and come to knowledge of the Truth". She understood the urgency of the universal mission, but when, like Saint Thérèse, she felt within her a desire for all vocations, including that of preaching to the ends of the earth, she never tried any means other than those given her by Jesus: suffering and the cross, offered in Love, in union with Him.

Her great joy remained the knowledge that her invisible offering was fruitful in the Mystical Body: "My suffering is bathed in the joy of my loving; for it is joyful since it comes from love, and since it is redemptive for souls... how infinitely sweet is the thought that, as a member of the Body of Christ, all my pain and sufferings, united to His loving sufferings, share in their divine efficacity".

She had a deep sense of the 'price' of each soul and the desire to save every one, by drawing many generous souls after her. She always spoke in universal terms. With Jesus she experienced that solidarity with humankind which led Him to be 'made sin' for us (St Paul); and while retaining an acute sense of her own weakness and unworthiness, she was aware of bearing the sins of a multitude of people with Jesus. Like Jesus at the time of his Agony, she experienced the fear which borders on anguish, but each time she surged forward, putting her trust in the Virgin Mary and in the priestly power of her Father in God, who was always present to encourage her to persevere in her offering, and who never ceased from bearing it in the Holy Sacrifice of the Mass.

Marthe addressed the long prayers which poured from her in murmurs, and which were sometimes cries of distress or else ejaculations of love, mainly to God the Father, conscious of being united with Jesus in his sacrifice for sinners, making intercession for each one, with a special predilection for priests. She implored the Virgin Mary on behalf of France and the whole world. She called on the Holy Spirit for her spiritual Father, the Foyer, the retreatants, and for the whole Church. She constantly renewed her offering and her 'yes' of love, despite frequent attacks by the devil who used every means to discourage her, with an infinite confidence in the support of her 'Maman Chérie', whom she never stopped invoking and thanking. Thus she drew from the well of contemplation joy which was deeper than her pain.

"At every moment of my life I have the ardent and great desire to save souls, all souls, by loving Jesus to distraction; this springs from my heart wounded by charity...".

"The beloved hand which leads me so lovingly towards the heights of pain is also the all-powerful hand which defends and strengthens me against the attacks and the terrible rage of the enemy".

Meetings with Marthe

"On va prier..."

Such prayer, such an offering, such self-giving could not but bear fruit. Marthe lived the mystery of the Communion of Saints in her hidden life, but also with those near her and those many visitors mysteriously attracted to her. Indeed, after becoming practically blind in 1940, having offered her sight to God for the end of the war, Marthe was like the suffering servant in Isaiah, "no looks to attract our eyes; a thing despised and rejected by men..." How can we explain the joy of children leaping around her divan, unless we see in her the presence of Him who said: "Let the little children come to me, for of such is the Kingdom of Heaven".

There was no room here for the self-satisfied, nor for the worldly or the curious. But little people, the poor in spirit, sinners, souls in search of truth, light, and a more generous life-style, it was these who came to Marthe and allowed themselves to be overwhelmed by her reception of them, during which she listened so simply to their problems. They left her strengthened by a certainty that thenceforward they would be 'taken in charge' by a faithful friend, a sure witness to God's faithfulness. Often the meeting had only lasted a few minutes. Many are those who bear witness to her influence, from old prison lags to the founders of religious orders.

Yet Marthe never proposed an easy solution to problems. She listened carefully; sometimes she simply kept silence. She prayed, and invited her visitors to pray with her. As a special treasure she would offer some saying of Jesus which came from her heart. She showed understanding and compassion so that the other person, feeling loved and respected and capable of being forgiven, and still more of becoming the saint that God expects, regained Hope. She was careful to direct the sinner towards a priest who in the sacrament of reconciliation could give him the fullness of God's tenderness.

She was always solicitous for the well-being of her guests. With great care and interest she supervised the contents of the parcels destined for missionaries, and still more for prisoners. At the same time she could be quite firm and demanding, with a clarity of vision based on sound common sense in which humour often played a part. For Marthe knew how to laugh with her visitors and to communicate her deep joy to them.

Often, by some small remark or precise question, she would face her visitor with his problem, but always with great delicacy, inviting him to reflect on his concrete situation and state of life. She knew that at the origin of many of our troubles there is the lazy avoidance of using our human capacity for reflection: "The earth is desolate because no one reflects".

To those who were suffering and indeed to everyone else, she would recall the value of that offering of self which she herself was living: "Each loving soul should be given an apostolic value to his life and sufferings, a redemptive value lasting to Eternity. More than ever the world needs holy and generous souls who, like living hosts, devote themselves entirely to self-sacrifice and to being victims of love".

One is struck by the humanity and balance of this woman, who quite clearly could not be sustained by her convictions alone, but rather by a personal relationship with her God: "I know that my God upholds me and looks at me always. This thought, which is a certainty, makes me happy and relaxed".

It was this profound and exciting 'science' of God's Mystery, fruit of the Holy Spirit, which transforms our outlook on the events of our daily lives, that she wanted to communicate to everyone: "Oh the untold greatness of the Christian life! In what captivating beauty, what an ocean of love, we live. Is it possible that God loves us to this extent?!"

Her earthly family also shared in her offering. In November 1940 Marthe took upon herself the pain of her dear mother's Purgatory for several months.

Who can estimate the many graces obtained during these meetings at 'La Plaine'? Marthe never forgot the people she met, nor those many who wrote to her letters which she always answered personally (via a secretary). All of them became involved in her weekly Passion. "On va prier" she used to say at the conclusion of a visit; but few may have suspected the weight of suffering covered by these words. For she never talked about what she was enduring. She lived faithfully that "gift of self to one and all in a complete giving to God". Her joy was to help others in a total forgetfulness of herself. As she said of the Virgin Mary, her constant preoccupation was "to bring to Jesus all those who came to her".

"My adorable Jesus. You who live in me, You who direct me and instruct me, make all those who come to me leave consoled when they weep, uplifted when depressed, and happy for some days remembering my words, my looks, my smiles."

"It has been said somewhere that nobody is more missionary than a saint, even though he remained enclosed within four walls".

1948-1981: The long hidden life of Marthe

"I count more than ever on my Beloved Mother to keep me humble, docile, trustful and very small, so that God may be free within my soul..."

From 1948 onwards, Marthe concealed herself increasingly in a silent offering. She no longer dictated her prayers, nor even spoke them aloud; but Père Finet continued faithfully to exercise his ministry as a 'Father' at her side. The attacks of the devil became more and more violent, but the presence of the Blessed Virgin marked Marthe with a sweetness which was a sign of the resurrection already being lived at the heart of the Passion. During her last years, the days when she could receive visitors became more limited, yet still 'la petite Marthe', as members of the Foyer referred to her with affection, continued to receive tirelessly those who came to see her.

It was then, too, that the remarkable growth of the Foyers occurred; the work which had already spread in France, found a new expansion to all parts of the world, after the foundation of a new school for boys at Saint Bonnet, the neighbouring parish where Marthe had been baptised. In this was realised the promise made by Jesus to Marthe and Père Finet received a growing number of 'faithful and devoted collaborators to help him absolve, instruct and nourish souls'. Numerous lay men and women felt the call to live their baptismal vocation by consecrating their lives to the Lord in a Foyer.

This "new Pentecost of Love", promised by Jesus to Marthe (in the same words used by Pope John XXIII at the opening of the Second Vatican Council), confirmed the Foyers in their mission for the Church, and bore witness to the fruitfulness of the hidden offering made by Marthe. For this reason, too, Châteauneuf remains, and will remain, the Centre Foyer, and the source of unity for all the other Foyers.

"Send forth your Spirit and all shall be created, and You will renew the face of the earth..."

"Holy Spirit, God of love, come like a powerful wind into our cathedrals, our churches and chapels, into our cenacles, into the most luxurious houses as into the humblest dwellings. Fill the whole earth with Your light, Your consolation and Your love".

"Oh Jesus, would that one day it might be said that Your Love has consumed me, not by reason of my efforts but by the effect of Your all-powerful grace...! that I am not dead, but living for love of You... Oh my God, if You can give me such peace, if You can make me so happy on this earth, what will Heaven be like?".

February 1981: the death of Marthe

'Obscure and unknown, that will be my privilege in Heaven".

"Unless the grain of wheat falls on the ground and dies". During the night of 5-6 February, Marthe returned to the Father, stripped of every comfort, after a final struggle with the devil who wished to pursue her 'to the very end'.

Her funeral was celebrated in an atmosphere of great recollection and peace, marked by deep joy in faith of the Resurrection, in the presence of a huge crowd gathered from every part of the world and every class of person. Mgr. Marchand, Bishop of Valence, presided at the celebration and preached on the words of St John's Gospel (chap. 12) which came from his heart after a visit to Marthe's mortal remains at La Plaine: "unless a wheat grain falls on the ground and dies, it remains only a single grain; but if it dies it yields a rich harvest".

"The mystery of Jesus is the mystery of Marthe. We may give thanks for her sense and love of the Church; both the diocesan Church and the universal Church. Witnessing to the absolute wonder of God, she always wished to remain a daughter of the Church".

By underlining her sense and love of the Church, the Bishop of Valence stressed the fundamental missionary grace received by Marthe and the Foyers of Charity; a grace received in the steps of Saint Thérèse for the

Church and for the whole world. "She wished to live her life in discretion and humility, knowing perfectly well, and with great common sense, that Faith is not based on the sensational..."

For those who draw near to her heart she remains the sign of the presence of Mary of Nazareth, where the mystery of the Redemption of the world was being prepared and already realised, by means of an offering hidden under the appearance of quite ordinary actions.

In this sense is not Marthe a 'prophet' for the laity, on whom the Church counts particularly in our times, and who are called "not only to transform the world, but to sanctify it from within?"

"The most ordinary looking life", said Marthe, "must raise us to the summits of union and love. True holiness is contained principally in perfect Charity, and this perfection can be attained by everyone without extraordinary graces, without special gifts, and even and above all without remarkable good works, but by becoming with St Thérèse of the Child Jesus a 'little soul' entirely given over to Love... a praying and praising soul". Marthe's conclusion was: "All perfection is in love. All holiness is in humility".

I hope that this brief survey of Marthe's life, which essentially belonged to God, will shed some light on the truth of Abbé Faure's description of Marthe as "a chosen soul". If one thinks of the free choice of love given by God to this humble creature, as to many others from among those thought of as small and unimportant in the eyes of the world, then indeed she was 'chosen'.

But in the ways of God such a choice which the chosen one is called to ratify by saying 'yes', only makes sense in a loving service of the Church for the world. The most beautiful service rendered by Marthe was to call each one of us baptised Christians, like a kind of elder sister or close friend, to contemplate the unique gift made to us by the Father "in his benevolent design of love", for the building up of the Body of Christ; He who "chose us in Him before the creation of the world, to be saints and to be perfect in Love in His presence".

How pleased Marthe would be that we should regard her as she herself liked to regard the Virgin Mary, as being "more to be imitated than admired".

Prayer

Most Sacred Heart of Jesus, You showed Marthe your great Design of Love and Life, in order to draw to yourself those who seek You or have forgotten You, and so that her unceasing offering of compassion and mercy may lead to participation in a New Pentecost.

We pray that her beatification by the Church will serve to make You better known, O Living Word of Love and Peace, and that by the intercession of Mary we may follow her example and respond to the appeals of all our needy brethren.

Be pleased to hear the prayers which we offer You through your servant Marthe, that your joy and glory may be made manifest. Amen.

"Jesus chooses a feeble, small and humble soul, He takes it in his arms, He commits it to his Heart. If it understands, if it abandons itself to Him, He forms it in his image. The mission of little souls is so beautiful and touching. They receive from the Lord the divine secret of doing with Him silently, without praise or human reward, great things for his Love, and for Heaven."

(Those who think they have received graces or favours through the intercession of Marthe, are asked to write to: The Commission of Enquiry, Cause of Marthe Robin, B.P. 825, 26008 Valence, France).

THE FIRST FOYER OF CHARITY

by Martin Blake

On 10 February 1936 a young priest in his thirties named Georges Finet drove down from Lyon, where he was Director of Education for the diocese, to the village of Châteauneuf-de-Galaure in the Drôme foothills to visit a lady he had not met before. He carried in his car a hand-coloured picture of Mary, Mediatrix of All Graces, which a mutual friend had asked him to deliver to her. Later he was to say: "I thought I was taking Our Lady's picture to Marthe, but it was She who was bringing me!"

Marthe lived with her parents in a small farmhouse a mile from the village. Born in 1902, the youngest of five children, she had been bed-ridden since 1928, and from 1929 more or less paralysed. Already she had a reputation for living in the closest possible mystical union with Christ and his Mother, and in October 1930 she had been marked with the stigmata of his Passion, and every Friday relived his sufferings on the Cross.

Marthe and Père Finet

This meeting was to prove providential, for it led to a partnership between Marthe and Père Finet which would only be broken by her death in 1981, by which time there would be some sixty Foyers in five continents. In the course of three hours of conversation, Marthe convinced the Abbé Finet that his vocation lay in helping her. For the first hour they spoke of the Blessed Virgin and her role in the Church. Finet, who gave Marian conferences on the teaching of St Louis Grignion de Montfort, was astonished at the depth of her insights. At three o'clock she began to talk of the great events which were soon to occur in the world, some very painful (World War II?), others rich in graces (Vatican II?) She announced 'a new Pentecost of Love' which would be preceded by a renewal of the Church. This renewal would occur by means of the apostolate of the laity. "Lay people are going to have a very important role to play. They will be formed in communities, notably in Foyers of Light, Charity and Love". Thus she anticipated the Second Vatican Council, and the call to renewal by the next three popes.

Père Finet asked her to define a Foyer. "It will be something quite new in the Church. It will consist of consecrated lay persons, but will not be a religious order. A Foyer will be a great family, with a priest at its head and Our Lady as its Mother. The teaching that will be given during retreats will be lived by the community as a witness to its unity and prayer. The Foyers will radiate light throughout the entire world. They will be an answer from the Heart of Christ to the world after the material defeat of people and their satanic errors". She named communism and secularism and freemasonry amongst these errors. There would be an intervention by Our Lady, she said.

At 4 o'clock Marthe turned to the Abbé Finet and said: "Monsieur l'Abbé, I have a request to make to you, on behalf of God".

"What is that, Mademoiselle?"

"It is you who must come here to Châteauneuf and found the first Foyer of Charity".

"I, Mademoiselle? But I am not in this diocese. I am from Lyon!"

"What does that matter, since God wills it!"

"Ah! I beg your pardon... I hadn't thought of it like that! But what would I do?"

"Many things. Chiefly you would preach retreats".

"But I do not know how".

"You will learn!"

"Yes... I suppose three day retreats would be a good thing".

"No. In three days one doesn't change a soul. The Blessed Virgin asks for five whole days".

"I see! And to whom will these retreats be given?"

"To begin with to ladies and older girls".

"And what shall we do during the retreats? Workshops? Discussion groups?"

"No! The Blessed Virgin wants complete silence".

"You think I shall be able to keep ladies and girls in silence for five days?"

"Yes, since that is what Our Lady asks for".

"Ah! I'm sorry... I hadn't thought of that! But how shall we publicise these retreats?"

"The Blessed Virgin will see to that. Jesus will give extraordinary graces. You won't need a lot of publicity!"

"But where will these retreats take place?"

"In the girls' school".

"But we shall need beds... and a kitchen. Who will take on this work?"

"You!"

"But with what money?"

"Don't worry... the Blessed Virgin will see to it!"

"When should the first retreat happen?"

"On Monday, the 7th of September... it will last until the afternoon of Sunday, the 13th".

"I can't refuse; but I shall have to ask permission from my superiors..."

"Of course! You must remain under obedience".

Abbé Finet's superior, Mgr. Bornet agreed to let him go. So did the Vicar-General of Lyon. Finally his spiritual director, a professor of theology at the university, was enthusiastic for the idea. He had already met Marthe.

Foyers retreats

Thus the first retreat was conducted for thirty-three persons (all women), several of whom were to become permanent members of this original Foyer. Today there is room for 200 retreatants at Châteauneuf, besides a school for girls and another in the next village for boys and, of course, a growing community. Fifteen other Foyers have been established in France, and more than seventy world-wide in forty countries. Only the Holy Spirit could have created such a phenomenon. The members do not wear a uniform or take religious vows. They make a 'commit-ment'; having entered, few leave.

Marthe Robin, whose cause is well advanced in Rome, would appear to be for the second half of this cen-tury what St Thérèse was for the first half. And indeed the two women are closely linked. Whereas Thérèse died aged 24 and became known through her autobiography, Marthe lived to be 79 (she died in 1981) of which the greater part was spent entirely immobilised in a small room in her parents' house. Mystically united to Christ and his Mother, she was visited by most of the retreatants who came to Châteauneuf over a period of fifty years. It has been estimated that she may have met a hundred thousand people; each one waited in the little kitchen and was allowed ten minutes with Marthe in her darkened room. She showed a keen interest in the affairs of each visitor, gave sound advice, and always finished by pray-ing with him or her. She had extraordinary insight into those who sought her advice, and all left her the better for their visit. A number of growing communities origi-nating in France, such as the Congregation of Saint John and the Community of the Beatitudes, owe their foundations partly to her support.

She left a large collection of prayers, meditations and observations (but she could not actually write herself), which are gradually being published, and a large number of books have been written about her. She is constantly quoted in the Foyers. As yet there is practically nothing in English, and we await the foundation of the first Foyer in the United Kingdom. Perhaps her most striking spiritual document was the Act of Consecration made in 1925 at the age of 23. In this masterpiece of spiritual thought the word 'love' appears twenty-two times, but 'justice' not once. From then on she was consecrated through Mary to Jesus to be a living sacrifice to God. The first full biography of Marthe by Raymond Peyret (who never met her) was entitled, *"Take my life Lord"* and subtitled, *'The Long Mass of Marthe Robin'*. She never attended Mass after 1928, yet her whole life was like a Mass, a perfect oblation of thanksgiving, united to the sacrifice of Christ on the Cross, inspired by love.

"One can only make people love to the extent that one possesses it, just as one can only radiate light if one carries within oneself the truth which is light".

(*Marthe Robin 16/2/30*)

SOME PRAYERS COMPOSED BY MARTHE ROBIN

Anima Christi

O Lord my God, while I am nourished each day by your Sacred Body, washed by your Redeeming Blood, enriched by your Holy Soul, flooded by your Divinity, may I love, desire, search for, wish for, and taste only You.

Let my heart and my whole being sigh for You alone, that I may be all yours and concerned only for You; that I may dwell perpetually with You, in You and united to You, in order that I may be entirely consumed in the ardent furnace of your Divine Heart. May I also be united as a child to the Immaculate Heart of my beloved Mother, with whom I want to glorify, praise, serve and obey You forever.

At Christmas Time

Divine Child Jesus, have pity on people who are all alone; have pity on lonely souls. Take care of them all and gather them to yourself on this evening's Feast, this night of Love, this dawn of peace and hope; so that their pain-filled hearts and troubled minds may find a refuge with their most loving, tender, all-powerful and true friend.

If I can feel them huddled near You, O my King, all my sufferings will melt away, forgotten in love.

Holy Child of the manger, who brings blessings and joy to the world, come into the souls who await You, who call to You, and make your heavenly dwelling within them, the house of your rest, your blessed manger.

All for the Love of God

Lord, I am ready to receive from your hand a more crushing cross and more lacerating sufferings if that is your will.

I want to ransom souls, not with gold or silver, but with the small change of my sufferings united with the inexhaustible treasure of the sufferings of the Redeemer and of his most Holy Mother, by the powerful means of the Cross, which is put at my disposal through the daily offering and silent immolation of my life to the Creator, who has given it to me. God is my Father, my Brother, and my special Friend, and from the moment that I became his child, his sister and his servant, nothing but nothing at all will happen to me, and I shall have nothing to suffer or undergo and nothing to endure, without as a good Father his having allowed and prepared it in advance.

An Offering of Trials

O Jesus, You are God and your love led You to become a man. The God-Man!

O Jesus, You have given your life freely for us. I beseech You to allow us to suffer and die like You, not as slaves or because we are obliged to, but freely and lovingly.

You have said there is no greater proof of love than to lay down one's life for a friend. Allow us to imitate You in our trials, in sickness, and at our death, that it may be an act of generosity to your greater glory and to your greater love. Better still, may it be an act of abandon and love.

O my God, may my sufferings be useful for my parents, for my friends and benefactors, for all Christians, for poor sinners, for the unbelievers, the proud and the persecutors, for my dear parishes and my noble country, for the whole of humanity which belongs to God. I want to die, not through feebleness or grief, not on account of illness, but like Jesus and with Jesus to die for love. Let my sickness be love!

Prayer of Abandonment

My God, take my memory and all its recollections; take my heart and all its affections; take my understanding and all its faculties; make them serve only for your greater Glory. Take my entire will, and I will merge it in yours. No longer what I want, O most sweet Jesus, but always whatever You want. Take me... receive me... direct me. Be my guide. I abandon myself entirely to You. I give myself to You a little host of Love, Praise and Thanksgiving, for the Glory of your Holy Name, for the enjoyment of your Love, for the triumph of your Sacred Heart, and for the perfect accomplishment of all your designs in me and around me.

O Blessed Virgin!

My divine Mother; give me your eyes so pure that I may contemplate Jesus. Give me your heart that I may love him. Engrave deeply on my soul the painful yet reassuring image of his Passion and glorious Resurrection, so that always having Jesus present in my mind and in my heart I may live until my death a life which is holy and pure and humble and hidden in God with Jesus and you, my good Mother.

Prayer for a Conversion

Dear Lord, please pray and offer yourself in me and in my place for this soul who is so dear to me and whom I entrust to you.

Dear God, please look after her and her affairs. I rely on you with confident hope and believe in your Love for us both. Accept my intentions, prayers and requests; my suffering, my offering and all my love.

O Jesus, you can see the eagerness with which I desire this conversion, this blessing, this grace. Please do not keep me waiting!

O Jesus, my God, through Mary my beloved Mother I leave all my desire with you and rest in your Love, being content to offer myself to you on behalf of this soul, certain that you will indicate to me whatever I can do; for I know you will care for her and for all my requests, and that you will soon do what is best for your Glory, and for all other souls.

Daily Prayers in the Foyers of Charity

The Angelus

The Angel of the Lord declared unto Mary
And she conceived of the Holy Spirit. *Hail Mary...*

Behold the handmaid of the Lord.
Be it done unto me according to thy word. *Hail Mary...*

And the Word was made flesh
And dwelt amongst us. *Hail Mary...*

Pray for us, O Holy Mother of God.
That we may be made worthy of the promises of
Christ. Pour forth, we beseech Thee, O Lord, Thy
grace into our hearts, that we to whom the Incarnation
of Christ thy Son was made known by the message of
an angel, may by his Passion and Cross be brought into
the glory of his Resurrection; through the same Christ
Our Lord. Amen.

Consecration to Mary

I choose you today, Mary, in the presence of the angels
and saints of heaven, for my Mother and Queen. I consecrate to you, in obedience and love, all that I am, all that I

have, and all the good that I may do, putting myself and all that belongs to me entirely at your service, for the greater glory of God in time and in eternity.

Prayer to Saint Joseph

Glorious Saint Joseph, head of the Holy Family of Nazareth, and so zealous in providing for all its needs, extend your tender care over all the Foyers of Charity, their Fathers, their members and their friends. Take under your guidance all their spiritual and temporal needs. And let their end be for the glory of God and the salvation of souls.

Prayer to Our Lady

Beloved Mother, you who know so well the paths of holiness and love, teach us to lift our minds and our hearts often to God, and to fix our respectful and loving attention on the Trinity. And since you walk with us on the path of eternal life, do not remain a stranger to the weak pilgrims your charity is ready to welcome. Turn your merciful face to us. Draw us into your light. Flood us with your kindnesses. Take us into the light and the love. Always take us further and higher into the splendours of heaven. Let nothing ever trouble our peace, nor turn us from the thought of God. But let each minute take us further into the depths of the awesome mystery, till the day when our souls - fully receptive to the light of the divine union - will see all things in eternal love and unity. Amen.

A Retreat in a Foyer of Charity

by Martin Blake

What are the Foyers?

There are nearly seventy Foyers of Charity spread throughout the world. All have been founded since 1936. They all have the same mission: to renew the Church by forming lay people. They reveal the dynamic work of the Holy Spirit who, we are told, "will renew the face of the earth".

What are the Foyers and how did they originate? The Canonical Structures approved by the Pontifical Council for the Laity in November 1986 define them thus:

"The Foyers of Charity are communities of baptised men and women who, following the example of the early Christians, share in common their material, intellectual and spiritual goods, and undertake to live together in the same spirit in order to bring about, with Mary as their Mother, the Family of God on earth, under the guidance of a priest, the Father, in a continuous effort of charity between themselves. By their life of prayer and work in the world they bear witness to Light, Charity and Love, according to the great message of Christ, King, Prophet and Priest".

The first Foyer

The first Foyer was started in a large manor house in a village called Châteauneuf-de-Galaure, south of Lyon.

In 1936 a young priest from Lyon, named Georges Finet met Marthe Robin. In three hours of conversation she prepared him for a challenge: that Our Lord wanted him to found the first Foyer of Charity and conduct five day silent retreats. His superiors gave him permission, and the first retreat was held in the château, which had already become a school. The link between school and Foyer, children and grown-ups was there from the beginning, and was always stressed by Marthe. Many of the Foyers now run a school as well as a retreat house.

A Foyer retreat

The retreat which I and three other English people followed at Courset, a mere fifteen miles inland from Boulogne, and so very accessible to England, was typical of a retreat in any of the seventy Foyers, though obviously there will be local variations. On our arrival we were greeted with tea or coffee and shown to our comfortable single or double rooms, purpose-built a few years ago, each with its own wash place, W.C. and shower. At 6.30 we assembled in the chapel, the upper part of a cleverly converted stable-block of the mid-19th Century country house which forms the nucleus of the Foyer. After being greeted by Père Tierny who founded the Foyer twenty five years ago, the retreatants joined with the community in adoring the Blessed Sacrament and receiving Benediction. We then moved downstairs to a large covered area between house and stable known as 'La Terrasse', where about 150 of the 200 school children were assembled sitting on the carpets, surrounded by thirty or forty chairs on which we sat. A touching ceremony followed in which Père Tierny got each visitor to introduce him or herself, after which an appointed child emerged from the throng who would become a sort of godchild for the week and form a prayer link with that grown-up. Mine was a charming nine year old called Benoit, whom I met on three occasions.

We then had our first meal, a four-course wholesome affair, taken in silence at round tables for eight, with classical music playing over the speakers. The food was beautifully cooked and served, and I noticed that special diets and fads were carefully catered for. Evening Prayer concluded the day, and we retired thankfully to our warm rooms.

Daily routine

Next morning began the routine which we were to follow for five days. We were wakened by music playing in the corridors at 7.30 and half-an-hour later we were at Morning Prayer in the chapel. This was conducted by 'Le Père' with leisurely pace, commenting on each psalm and giving us thoughts for the day. The instrument which accompanied hymns and psalms was a zither, highly suitable for a fairly confined space. The altar is a massive oval piece of polished wood. A simple tabernacle is set against the wall behind it, with a Russian icon of Our Lady hanging nearby. Chair's extend in rows of seven the length of the chapel and a couple of rows are set along the right-hand side.

Eight-thirty and the bell sounds for petit déjeuner, coffee or tea with the usual bread, butter and jam. At 9.15 we assemble in the conference room below the Chapel. Both are in strikingly good taste, like everything in the Foyer, their walls lined with coconut fibre. We sit at tables for four with bibles and note-books at the ready. First a brief practice of the chants for the day at Mass and Evening Prayer. Then Père Tierny arrives and begins with a 'Réjouis-toi, Marie, comblée de grace...', a nice variation of the old 'Je vous salue, Marie...' He then launches into an hour of brilliant commentary on the chosen theme, apparently without a note, illustrated with New Testament texts, filled with valuable insights, and spiced with personal reminiscences and digressions. This pattern is to be maintained for three sessions each day for five days. The solid formation given by such rich fare is the hallmark of all the Foyers, as Marthe intended, but I cannot help feeling that the conferences are at their very best at Courset. It was noticeable how frequently Père Tierny quoted Marthe. Another he mentioned several times was Cardinal Newman.

The daily Mass was at 11.15. Père Tierny concelebrated with two other priests. At each of three of the masses there was a group of children from the school, and at the homily time Père Tierny gave us a skillful demonstration of teaching methods as he involved the children in the thought process by means of question and answer. How well those youngsters had been taught; and with what love and evident joy they were lapping up the Faith; one felt they must surely already be committed to the Lord's service for life. Marthe had shown the value of children in the life of a Foyer: here was tangible evidence of this fact. "Unless you become as children you cannot enter the Kingdom of God".

Those who have criticised the reformed Roman Rite of Paul IV should waste no more time but go to a Foyer. There they will find that the new rite is far richer, more meaningful, more involving, more loving and more prayerful than the old 'Tridentine Rite' could ever be.

Lunch follows the Mass, and a strong 'cidre bouchée' is drunk, the nectar of the north. After a break comes the afternoon talk, and then a beautiful rosary conducted in 'La Terrasse'. This too involves groups of the children who remain for one or two decades. Another break is followed by a 'goûtier' and at 5.45 the third instruction. From this we return upstairs to the Chapel for an hour's silent prayer before the exposed Blessed Sacrament. Here we have a chance to continue savouring the graces of our morning

Communion, to share the presence of our Blessed Lord with the other retreatants and community members, and to pray for the intentions which we and the children have written on pieces of paper and placed in the basket at the foot of the altar. What the French call 'un temps fort' indeed.

Next comes supper - no cider or coffee - and we are free until Evening Prayer ends the day at 9.15. I should mention one detail common to all the Foyers, namely a large basket marked 'Corbeille de Marthe'. In her lifetime Marthe was most solicitous in sending help to those who were in real need, particularly prisoners and the young Foyers in the third-world countries. With her helpers she collected, packed and despatched innumerable parcels. This custom continues, and into Marthe's basket go packets of cigarettes, bars of chocolate, cakes of soap, Bibles, prayer books and rosaries, and other small gifts which are then parcelled and sent to prisons or poor Foyers.

This Foyer has over two hundred children in its school, nearly forty members in the community, and it can accommodate as many as two hundred retreatants during holiday time or one hundred during term time. At Châteauneuf you can treble those school figures and add an agricultural college for women and a home for the elderly. This evident renewal of the Church which was initiated just before World War II, when Marthe foresaw a 'new Pentecost of Love', is no small-scale affair. The sooner we get a Foyer or two going in the British Isles, the better it will be for us all.

Here are the addresses of some of the Foyers:

Foyer de Charité B.P. 11,
26330 Châteauneuf-de-Galaure, Drôme.

B.P. 105, 62240 Courset, Pas-de-Calais.

Tressaint, B.P. 145, 22104 Dinan, Côtes-du-Nord.

"La Flatière", 74310 Les Houches, Haute-Savoie.

4900 Spa (Nivèze), Belgium.

74 Hollett Street, North Scituate, Mass 02060, USA.

"Villa Châteauneuf", C.P. 298, Sutton (P.Q.) Canada.

Further Reading and Information

There are a number of French-language studies of Marthe Robin, of which the fullest is R. Peyret, **Prends ma Vie, Seigeur: La Longue Messe de Marthe Robin** (Desclee de Brower, 1985). Another of Père Peyret's books has been published in an English translation: R. Peyret, **Marthe Robin: The Cross and the Joy** (Alba House, 1983).

There are three Associations of Friends of the Foyers in the British Isles. Those interested in learning more about the Foyers of Charity should write to:

Irish Friends of the Foyers
24 Maple Road,
Clonskeagh,
Dublin 14 Ireland

Scottish Friends of the Foyers
77 University Road,
Old Aberdeen
AB2 3DR

English Friends of the Foyers
4 Dunkerton Close
Glastonbury
BA6 8LZ

Informative Catholic Reading

We hope that you have enjoyed reading this booklet.

If you would like to find out more about CTS booklets - we'll send you our free information pack and catalogue.

Please send us your details:

Name ....

Address ....

....

....

Postcode ....

Telephone ....

Email ....

Send to: CTS, 40-46 Harleyford Road,
            Vauxhall, London
            SE11 5AY

Tel: 020 7640 0042
Fax: 020 7640 0046
Email: info@cts-online.org.uk

 **CTS**